KU-689-852

Eric Thompson was weaned on good Scottish humour in a family where laughter took pride of place. He began writing comic verse whilst still at primary school and when he joined the Navy, it was only a matter of time before he was being asked to perform at Burns Suppers and other Naval dinners.

Through this, he developed the habit of writing comic tales, usually in verse, to embellish his speeches. He is one of the few writers to have performed his work whilst on patrol in a submarine. Since leaving the Navy, he has entertained audiences at venues ranging from the London Hilton to Glasgow comedy clubs.

In 1996, he won the BBC Radio Scotland Burns Bicentenary poetry writing prize for his hilarious tale of 'Ally Shanter', which he also performed at the first Glasgow International Festival of Comedy in 2003.

In 2002, he was commissioned to write the 'Helensburgh Bicentenary Poem' which received a standing ovation when performed at the town's Bicentenary celebrations. Now, after many years of live performance, he has decided to publish his party pieces.

'Colquhounsville-sur-Mer' is his first of the published collections.

Contents

Notes

'The Helensburgh Bicentenary Poem' was first performed in the Victoria Halls, Helensburgh on 28th July, 2002. The poem was published informally in the Helensburgh Advertiser and in the Helensburgh Heritage Society's Newsletter. It is now filed in the official archives of Argyll & Bute Council. 'The Wreck of the Sugar Ship' and 'The Waverley' were written and performed during a McGonagall Supper organised by the 1st Craigendoran Venture Scouts.

'Noah's Comet' was written for and performed at the 75th Anniversary of the Scottish Branch of the Institute of Marine Engineers in The Thistle Hotel, Glasgow, and subsequently performed at 'Sing for your Supper' in the Victoria Halls, Helensburgh. It has been published informally in the Helensburgh Advertiser and in the Journal of the Institute of Marine Engineers. 'Rule of the Road' and 'Anti-Submarine Protest' were first performed at the 1997 Cove Sailing Club annual dinner. 'The Twa Dogs o' Faslane' was first performed at a Burns Supper in the Wardroom (officers' mess) in the Clyde Submarine Base, Faslane, whilst the author was serving as a Commander in the Third Submarine Squadron. 'A Wife, a Yacht, and a Bottle of Gin' was written for and performed at the 1996 annual dinner of the Gareloch Owners' Association, the 'Gareloch' being a local class of traditional wooden yacht.

A Brief History of Helensburgh

In AD 142, the Roman Emperor Antoninus built the Antonine wall which ran from Old Kilpatrick on the Clyde to Bo'ness on the Forth. In the Roman mappa mundae, this wall defined the limit of the civilized world and so Dumbarton, Strathclyde's ancient capital, was classed officially as uncivilized. As recently as the eighteenth century, there were still no roads into the wilderness beyond Dumbarton. However, one of the lairds of Loch Lomondside then decided to think big.

In 1740, Sir James Colquhoun, 26th Laird of Luss, 1st Baronet of Great Britain, and progenitor of 'Take the High Road', married Lady Helen Sutherland, granddaughter of the Duke of Sutherland. Five years later, Scotland convulsed in the ruinous Jacobite uprising of 1745. 14 years later, Robert Burns was born and six years after that, up the Clyde in Glasgow, James Watt invented the world's first efficient steam engine. The following year, 1776, the colony of America declared its independence and in that same year, for reasons best known to himself, Sir James Colqhuoun decided to build a new industrial town in the wilderness. This became what we now know as Helensburgh.

In 2002, Helensburgh celebrated the bicentenary of its burgh status and the Bicentenary Poem was commissioned to mark the occasion. Amongst other things, the poem resolves the unexplained mystery of why Sir James Colquhoun decided to build an industrial town in such a remote place. The poem was first performed at the bicentenary lunch in the Victoria Halls, Helensburgh, on 28th July 2002, 200 years to the day after King George III granted the town its Royal Charter.

THE HELENSBURGH BICENTENARY POEM

Colquhoun stabbed the haggis wi' his bluntit skean dhu,

Then grabbed his Factor by the throat and begged him what to do.

'I'm cruising for a bruising, man! I'm heading for a rift.

'It's Lady Helen's birthday and I havnae bought a gift!'

The Factor scratched his sporran. His brain was running hot.

'Why no gie'r a toun on a' that rubbish land you've got?'

'Man! Man! That's pure ded brilliant. You are a genius!

'Ah'll build it on Loch Lomondside and ca' the new place Luss.'

'Naw, naw,' the Factor cried. 'Ah meant ower by the Clyde.

'Malig's just the place tae build a new toun fur yur bride.'

'By the sea! Colquhounsville-sur-mer! She'll be ower the moon!'

'Naw, naw, Sir James!' the Factor groaned. 'You'll call it Helenstoun.'

COLQUHOUNSVILLE - SUR - MER
Helenstoun

Colquhoun grabbed the haggis and some Irn Bru to toast her,

Then rushed to Lady Helen who slept deep in her four poster.

'I'm gie'in' you a toun,' he roared, then kissed her on the lips.

She fixed him with her bleary eyes and whispered, 'Where's the chips?'

The planners planned a town to bring in industry and traders,

With ferries on the seafront and arcades for space invaders.

This was to be a working town with all the newest fangles

And, just to keep it tidy, all the streets were at right angles.

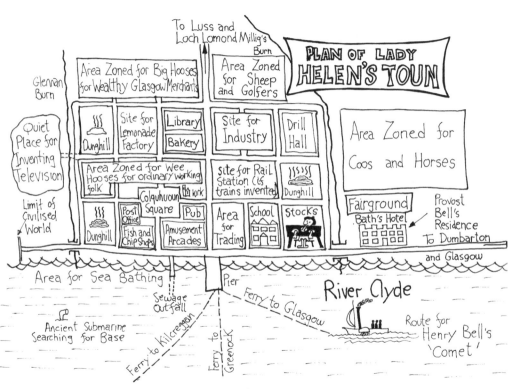

To Luss and
Loch Lomond

Millig's Burn

PLAN OF LADY HELEN'S TOUN

Glennan Burn

Area Zoned for Big Hooses for Wealthy Glasgow Merchants

Area Zoned for Sheep and Golfers

Quiet Place for Inventing Television

Dunghill

Site for Lemonade Factory

Library

Bakery

Site for Industry

Drill Hall

Area Zoned for Coos and Horses

Limit of Civilised World

Area Zoned for Wee Hooses for ordinary working folk

Colquhuoun Square

Kirk

Post Office

Pub

site for Rail Station (5 trains invented)

Dunghill

Dunghill

Fish and Chip Shops

Amusement Arcades

Area for Trading

School

Stocks

Fairground

Bath's Hotel

Provost Bell's Residence

To Dumbarton and Glasgow

Area for Sea Bathing

Sewage Outfall

Pier

Ferry to Glasgow

River Clyde

Ancient Submarine Searching for Base

Ferry to Kilcreggan

Ferry to Greenock

Route for Henry Bell's 'Comet'

9

But trade came slow. It failed to grow. So, twenty six years later,
The folks all racked their brains on how to make their wee place greater.
They sought a vision for the town with business plans more thorough,
And, just to up its status, sought the Charter for a Burgh.

The King gie'd the Charter Royal in Eighteen Hunnerd and Two
When Helen's town became a Burgh wi' Crest and Council too.
Wi' Provost, Town Clerk, Baillies twa, and Cooncillors by four,
It wisnae quite the jackpot but it opened up a door.

The Charter granted rights to hold four annual fairs and market
So folks would bring their cart to town - and then get charged to park it.
It granted rights to rid the town of dunghills and of prowling
And stick those owners in the stocks whose dogs had been caught fouling.

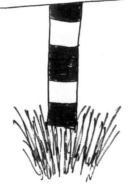

HELENSTOUN BURGH

The Town Clerk called the folk to name, for popular election,
A Provost who would give the town a sense of new direction.
When one wag cried, 'Gie's King Billy', the Clerk glowered o'er his lorgnette.
'Ye cannae have King Billy, for Petrie's[1] no been born yet!'

'Twas Henry Bell of the Baths Hotel became the Provost first
And, on finding all the coffers bare, he poked the Clerk and cursed.
'We'll no survive on Council Tax from farms and shops and bakers.
'If this Burgh is to thrive, we'll need the holidaymakers.'

So, Provost Bell applied his brain to business-led invention
Then put an engine in his boat, defying all convention.
Five hours and more from Glasgow town, a horsedrawn coach would clatter,
But Henry Bell had figured it was quicker 'doon the watter'.

(1. Councillor Billy Petrie, Convenor of Argyll & Bute Council in 2002)

The tourist trade then prospered thanks to steamships on the Clyde
And wealthy Glasgow merchants came to Helensburgh tae bide.
But history shows this tourist boom was really rather brief
For by the new millenium, folks flew to Tenerife.

Now, in this bicentenary of Lady Helen's Burgh,
The town is looking back but needs to plough another furrow.
No Provost, Baillies, Town Clerk now. The tourism is in wither.
It's time again for Helensburgh to get its act together.

IN THE STYLE OF WILLIAN McGONAGALL

THE WRECK OF THE SUGAR SHIP

O great sugar ship on the River Clyde

Lying dead like a great whale on your side.

It was one tragic winter gale that you dragged your anchor

And the shipping company called your Captain an 'Effing W..nker'.

THE WAVERLEY

The Waverley is a beautiful paddle boat

Which into Helensburgh brings lots of trade

And many tourists from her walk up Sinclair Street

Right up as far as the Glade.

As they return downhill at night the blisters on their feet are burning

And when they reach the pier they're sick as parrots to find

The Waverley has been and gone and won't be returning.

A BRIEF PIECE OF MARITIME HISTORY

The Clyde is the birthplace of the world's steamship industry and history relates that it was Henry Bell, first Provost of the new town of Helensburgh, who built the world's first seagoing steamship. Bell's 'Comet' was built to transport tourists from Glasgow to Helensburgh, passing the ancient fortress of Dumbarton en route, and it began the seagoing industrial revolution. However, students of the Bible have argued that the 'Comet' was in fact an act of God, or his agent Noah...............

NOAH'S COMET

Noah built an ark although there wisnae any watter,
Prompting all his mates to cry,
'Haw, Noah, whit's the matter?'
'Ah've hud a sign frae Goad,' he said,
'The watter's on its way!'
Consumed wi' fear, they shoutit back,
'Will we all huv tae pay?'
'Naw! Naw!' Noah said,
'This stuff's no for drinkin'.
'This is what you call a flood.
'The kind of stuff you sink in!
'That's why ah've built masel' this ark.
'A hoose up on a boat.
'So when the watter reaches here,
'Me and the wife can float.'

A hush descended on the throng.

They knew not what he meant

How tae build an ark

Was something only Noah kent.

But Noah's brother, Know-All, tapped the hull

And gied a shudder.

'If this ark's meant tae be a boat,

'It hasnae got a rudder!'

Noah scanned his ark at length
And glowered wi' deep concern.
He'd built a bow at both its ends
But hadnae built a stern.
He sighed out loud wi' heavy heart.
His jaw fell tae his chest.
He'd nicked the plans frae Yarrows
'Cos he thought they were the best.
'Ah built this from a drawing,' he groaned.
'Ah wis gettin' on just fine
'But Ah never made allowance for
'A Ministry design!'

Enraged he shoutit up tae Goad
'It's enough tae mak ye spit.
'Here's me trying tae be scientific
'And Ah'm made tae look a twit.'

At that the heavens opened
And doon the watter gushed,
Drownin' a' his friends
Which Noah didnae think was just.
For he was safe upon the waves,
His trusty ark had floatit,
And so he cracked a can of beer
Determined tae get stoatit.

When Noah's wife came up on deck,
Feeling no too grand,
She saw the flood and roared,
'Haw Noah, where the hell's the land?'
She gazed at a' the watter
And at Noah gettin' drunk.
'Ah've just pit oot ma washin'
'And the whole damn lot has sunk!'

For forty days and forty nights,
Noah's wife kept thinking.
'Noah, seein' as how we're lost at sea,
'Is it no time you stopped drinking?'

Noah poured another beer
And gie'd the question thought.
He thought of a' the options
None o' which he'd really got.
'As we huvnae got an engine
'Or a rudder Ah can use,
'Ah think before Ah die
'Ah ought tae finish a' the booze.'

His wife put all her faith in Goad
Playing hymns on their piano
Until she couldnae stand the smell
Of bilges filled wi' guano
One day she shoutit in his ear,
'See you, ye idle pratt.
'Get aff your butt at once
'And clean up where the beasts huv shat.'

At that there was a mighty crash,
The beasts all ran amok.
Noah's ark had grounded
Halfway up Dumbarton Rock!
'This is an act of Goad,' he said,
'The Land o' Jamie Watt.
'Now Ah'll get an engine
'And the rudder Ah forgot!'

A man arrived frae Yarrow's,
Sent down by their Chief Exec,
Tae ask if he could gie a quote
For fixing Noah's wreck.
An engineer from Millig
Whose name was Henry Bell
Produced a large steam engine
Which he said he'd like to sell.
As there had never been a steamship
Noah saw another sign.
He said, 'Ah'll buy the engine
'But the patent must be mine.'
So Noah built a shipyard.
Put the engine in his ark.
Then steamed it doon the watter
Faster than the Cutty Sark.
When overtaking sailing ships,
Their skippers a' went pale.
They'd never seen a ship propelled
Which didnae have a sail.

The news soon spread tae Greenock
That something awfie queer
Was sailing doon the watter
And about tae reach their pier.
It had a mill wheel on each side
And for a mast, a lum!
Folk couldnae think from where
This apparition might have come.

As Noah hit the pier at speed
The engine's gasket blew
And tipped intae the watter
A' the men who formed his crew.

Noah climbed upon the pier

Tae calm the troubled throng.

'If you think Ah'm powered by magic,

'You're absolutely wrong.

'This Ark o' mine's a steamship.

'It is the world's first.'

'My voyage has been historic but -

'Ye huvnae heard the worst.

'The days of sail are over!

'A' your sails can now be furled.

'For this steamship, built by Noah,

'Will change the shipping world.'

He pointed proudly at his craft,
Then felt the urge tae vomit.
For Henry Bell had changed its name,
And called his Ark, 'The Comet'.

RULE OF THE ROAD

A nautical fellow called Gus

Towed his dinghy from Glasgow to Luss.

When he cornered too fast

The boat lost its mast

And the boom hit the Fort William bus.

ANTI-SUBMARINE PROTEST

A submarine sailing past Rhu

Ran over a Greenpeace canoe.

The Peace Camp proclaimed

Their canoeist was maimed

But he turned up next day on the buroo.

In his brilliant satire, 'The Twa Dogs', Robert Burns observed society through the eyes of two dogs, one, Caesar, being the laird's Labrador and the other, Luath, being the shepherd's collie. It requires only minor adjustment to reset the tale in the context of the nuclear submarine base at Faslane and its adjacent peace camp.

THE TWA DOGS O' FASLANE

'Twas in that place of Scotland's Pride

That bears the name of auld COMCLYDE[1]

Upon a bonnie day in June

When wearin' through the afternoon

Twa dogs, that werena missed frae hame

Foregathered once upon a time.

The first I'll name, they ca'd him Caesar,
Was keepit for the Commodore's pleasure;
His hair, his size, his mouth, his lugs,
Show'd he was none o' Scotland's dugs,
But came frae some place far abroad
Where sailors go to fish for cod.
His locked, letter'd, braw brass collar
Shew'd him the gentleman and scholar;
But though of highest pedigree,
Nae hint of pride, nae pride had he.
But wad hae talked wi full proprieties
To a' Heinz 57 varieties.
The other was a protester's collie,
A rhyming, ranting, Peace Camp wallie
Who for his friend and comrade had him
And in his freaks, had Luath ca'd him.
He was a rough and faithful tyke
As ever leapt a ditch or dyke.
His honest, sonsie, bawsent face
Aye gat him friends in ilka place.

Nae doubt these dogs were thick thegither
And unco fond o'one anither.
Wi' social noses, sniff and snuffle,
They'd watched the police and campers scuffle
Until wi' pleasure weary grown
Upon a knowe they sat them down
And there began a long digression
About the lords of the creation.

CAESAR

I've often wondered, honest Luath
What life poor Peace Camp dogs like you have.
The Navy life is such a skive
But how do Peace Camp folk survive?
COMCLYDE gets rich remuneration
And house supplied by gratefu' nation.
He rises when he likes himsel'
Whilst Reggies[2] give his ratings hell.

He calls his car, he calls his driver,
(Another state enlisted skiver),
And at the Base he turns up late
But's aye saluted at the gate!
     From morn till e'en the chefs are toiling
At baking, roasting, frying, boiling;
And though the Wardroom[3] eat like kings,
The junior rates are well fed things.
Police alsatians, blastit bullies,
Get food that floods there mooths wi' droolies
But what about a Camper's diet?
I'll vow my master wouldnae try it.

LUATH

Truth, Caesar, his life is tough.
His tents and vans are truly rough
But his is a Council aided mess
Subsidised by the DSS[4]

Himsel', and wife, he thus sustains
And now he's even having weans!
Ye must well think, a wee touch langer
And they must starve o' cold and hunger;
But how it comes, I never kent yet.
They're maistly wonderfu' contented.
Ah, hairy men and burly hussies
Are bred in such a way as this is.

CAESAR

But then to see how ye're neglected
How cuffed and kicked and disrespected.
Lord, man, COMCLYDE treats his yellow wellies
Wi' more respect than Peace Camp smellies.
I've noticed on their break-in days,
And they've breached yon fence in many ways,
Peace Camp laddies short o'cash,
Get apprehended just like trash

And ta'en away by Strathclyde Police
And fined for breachin' o' the peace!
I see how folk live that hae riches;
But surely Camp folk maun be wretches.

LUATH ·

They're no sae wretched's ane would think
Though constantly on breadline's brink.
They're sae accustomed to the fight
The Navy gi'es them little fright
An' though fatigued wi' unemployment
They find that rest's a sweet enjoyment.
They lay aside their private cares
For international affairs.
They sacrifice to gain attention
For Britain's good is their intention.

CAESAR

Haith, lad, ye little ken about it:
For Britain's good! - good grief! I doubt it.
Say rather, simple fools
Used as politicians' tools
Manipulated for the gain
Of leaders far from squalor's pain.
Who'd soon forget these faithful minions
To suit a shift in mass opinions.
Sheridan and Galloway!
They only turn up on the day
To get their photies in the press
Then leave you to your filthy mess.
Ha! For Peace on Earth with Trident trifle?
They'd also have to ban the rifle!

LUATH

        Hech man! Ten million pounds for yonder fence!
Is that what your lot call Defence?
But will you tell me, Master Caesar?
Sure Wardroom life's a life of pleasure.
Nae cauld nor hunger e'er need stir them.
The very thought o't needna' fear them.

CAESAR

        Lord, man, were ye whyles where I am
The Wardroom - ye wadnae envy them!
 It's true they neednae starve or sweat
Thro' winters cauld or summer's heat
They've nae rough work to craze their bones
And fill auld age wi' gripes and groans
But human bodies are such fools,
For a' their colleges and schools

That, when nae real ills perplex them,
They find the stress enough to vex them.
And aye the less they have tae pain them,
In like proportion, less will hurt them.
The gentlemen, and ladies worst,
Wi' downright want o' work are cursed.
They loiter, lounging, lank and lazy
With duties which are pretty hazy.
Their days insipid, dull and tasteless;
Their nights unquiet, long and restless
And e'en their sports, their balls and races,
Their gadding about in public places.
There's so much fuss, such pomp and art
The pleasures scarcely touch their heart.
The men dress up like high class dames
Then rip their clothes in daft mess games.
Ae night their mad wi' drink and whoring
Next day their life is past enduring.
            There's some exception, man and woman,
But this is Wardroom life in common.

By this the sun was out o'sight
And darker gloaming brought the night
When they got up and shook their lugs,
Rejoiced they werena men but dugs.
And each took off his separate way
Resolved to meet some other day.

1 COMCLYDE   Comander of the Faslane nuclear submarine base
2 Reggies   Naval Regulators (i.e. police)
3 Wardroom   Officers' Mess
4 DSS   Department of Social Security

THE WIFE, A YACHT AND A BOTTLE OF GIN
(In the style of Stanley Holloway)

A man with a well varnished Gareloch
Whose face was all wizened and thin,
Took passage from Shandon to Clynder
With his wife and a bottle of gin.

He tacked and he gybed and he shouted
In the teeth of a Northerly gale
Till his wife, seeing no sign of progress,
Advised him to put up a sail.

As he hoisted the main with a twist in,
From the foredeck, his faithful wife squealed.
"We havnae let go of the mooring!"
Then over to starboard they heeled.

Unleashed from the fetters of mooring,
The yacht made a run for the shore,
And the wife made a dive for the tiller,
Screaming, "I cannae take any more!"

"Ready about!" the wife ordered
As the boom it came flanging across.
And struck her old man on the forehead
As he roared out, "It's me that's the boss!"

He was felled to the deck like a dead man
His nose it were broken and numb,
While his wife at the tiller stood roaring,
She wished that she never had come.

His specs they were knocked to the bilges
Where he grappled to little avail.
So he called for his wife to, "do something,"
Like get out the bucket and bale.

At length in the murk of the cuddy,
His hand felt the bottle of gin
Which he drank all at once in a fervour
Then gazed at his wife with a grin.

He gazed from the bilge paralytic
Shouting nautical things at the sky
And laughing insanely at seagulls
Till one landed a shot in his eye.

All day his wife stood at that tiller
And fought with the wild, raging sea
Till, at sunset, she cried in a panic,
"I'll burst if I don't have a wee!"

So the bucket was passed to the cockpit
For the helmsman to have her relief
But with tiller and oilskins to cope with
The exercise ended in grief.

She were perched on the edge of that bucket,
With her cheeks full exposed to the breeze
And she piddled all over her trousers
Which were pulled halfway down to her knees.

"To hell with this sailing," she hollered,
"We're selling this boat in the Spring
"And in future if we're going sailing,
"It's not in this clinker built thing!"

"This 'thing', dearest wife, is a Gareloch,
"A yacht with a real touch of class.
"But the bucket I gave you to pee in
"Was too small for the size of your ass!"

So the man with the well varnished Gareloch,
Whose face was so wizened and thin,
Got rid of his wife in the Springtime
And just sails with his bottle of gin.

Now heed this advice all you sailors.
If you want to share wife with your yacht,
Make sure that it's got a nice toilet
That fits snug on the feminine bot!